*This Journal*
# BELONGS TO

_____

_____

 # My
# CHICKEN

*Place a Picture of Your Chicken Here*

# My
# CHICKEN

Name:

_____

_____

Breed/Type of Chicken:

_____

Date/Place of Purchase:

_____

Hen ☐                    Rooster ☐

Purpose: ☐Egg Layer  ☐Meat  ☐Pet  ☐Other

Description/Colors/Identifying Marks:

_____

_____

Known Age/Hatch Date:

_____

Diet/Feed Type:

_____

_____

Notes

_____

_____

 # My Chicken's
# HEALTH

### Health Record

Date:

Condition/Illness/Symptoms:

_____

_____

Treatment/Medication:

_____

_____

Changes in Behaviour:

_____

_____

Notes:

_____

_____

### Vet Check Up Appointments:

_____        _____

_____        _____

_____        _____

_____        _____

 # My Chicken's
# HEALTH

Health Record

Date:

Condition/Illness/Symptoms:

_____

_____

Treatment/Medication:

_____

_____

Changes in Behaviour:

_____

_____

Notes:

_____

_____

Vet Check Up Appointments:

_____        _____

_____        _____

_____        _____

_____        _____

# My Chicken's
# HEALTH

Health Record

Date:

Condition/Illness/Symptoms:

_____

_____

Treatment/Medication:

_____

_____

Changes in Behaviour:

_____

_____

Notes:

_____

_____

Vet Check Up Appointments:

_____        _____

_____        _____

_____        _____

_____        _____

# My Chicken's
# HEALTH

## Health Record

Date:

Condition/Illness/Symptoms:

_____

_____

Treatment/Medication:

_____

_____

Changes in Behaviour:

_____

_____

Notes:

_____

_____

## Vet Check Up Appointments:

_____        _____

_____        _____

_____        _____

_____        _____

# My Chicken's
# HEALTH

Health Record

Date:

Condition/Illness/Symptoms:

_____

_____

Treatment/Medication:

_____

_____

Changes in Behaviour:

_____

_____

Notes:

_____

_____

Vet Check Up Appointments:

_____        _____

_____        _____

_____        _____

_____        _____

# My Chicken's
# HEALTH

## Health Record

Date:

Condition/Illness/Symptoms:

_____

_____

Treatment/Medication:

_____

_____

Changes in Behaviour:

_____

_____

Notes:

_____

_____

## Vet Check Up Appointments:

_____          _____

_____          _____

_____          _____

_____          _____

 # My Chicken's
# HEALTH

Health Record

Date:

Condition/Illness/Symptoms:

_____

_____

Treatment/Medication:

_____

_____

Changes in Behaviour:

_____

_____

Notes:

_____

_____

Vet Check Up Appointments:

_____          _____

_____          _____

_____          _____

_____          _____

# My Chicken's
# HEALTH

Health Record

Date:

Condition/Illness/Symptoms:

_____

_____

Treatment/Medication:

_____

_____

Changes in Behaviour:

_____

_____

Notes:

_____

_____

Vet Check Up Appointments:

_____          _____

_____          _____

_____          _____

_____          _____

# My Chicken's
# HEALTH

Health Record

Date:

Condition/Illness/Symptoms:

_____

_____

Treatment/Medication:

_____

_____

Changes in Behaviour:

_____

_____

Notes:

_____

_____

Vet Check Up Appointments:

_____        _____

_____        _____

_____        _____

_____        _____

# My Chicken's
# HEALTH

Health Record

Date:

Condition/Illness/Symptoms:

_____

_____

Treatment/Medication:

_____

_____

Changes in Behaviour:

_____

_____

Notes:

_____

_____

Vet Check Up Appointments:

_____          _____

_____          _____

_____          _____

_____          _____

# Notes &
# OBSERVATIONS

---

---

---

---

---

---

---

---

---

---

---

---

---

---

 # My
# CHICKEN

*Place a Picture of Your Chicken Here*

# My
# CHICKEN

Name:

_____

_____

Breed/Type of Chicken:

_____

Date/Place of Purchase:

_____

Hen ☐                                    Rooster ☐

Purpose: ☐Egg Layer   ☐Meat   ☐Pet   ☐Other

Description/Colors/Identifying Marks:

_____

_____

Known Age/Hatch Date:

_____

Diet/Feed Type:

_____

_____

Notes

_____

_____

_____

# My Chicken's
# HEALTH

## Health Record

Date:

Condition/Illness/Symptoms:

_____

_____

Treatment/Medication:

_____

_____

Changes in Behaviour:

_____

_____

Notes:

_____

_____

## Vet Check Up Appointments:

_____          _____

_____          _____

_____          _____

_____          _____

# My Chicken's
# HEALTH

Health Record

Date:

Condition/Illness/Symptoms:

_____

_____

Treatment/Medication:

_____

_____

Changes in Behaviour:

_____

_____

Notes:

_____

_____

Vet Check Up Appointments:

_____        _____

_____        _____

_____        _____

_____        _____

# My Chicken's
# HEALTH

## Health Record

Date:

Condition/Illness/Symptoms:

_____

_____

Treatment/Medication:

_____

_____

Changes in Behaviour:

_____

_____

Notes:

_____

_____

## Vet Check Up Appointments:

_____        _____

_____        _____

_____        _____

_____        _____

 # My Chicken's
# HEALTH

Health Record

Date:

Condition/Illness/Symptoms:

_____

_____

Treatment/Medication:

_____

_____

Changes in Behaviour:

_____

_____

Notes:

_____

_____

Vet Check Up Appointments:

_____     _____

_____     _____

_____     _____

_____     _____

# My Chicken's
# HEALTH

### Health Record

Date:

Condition/Illness/Symptoms:

_____

_____

Treatment/Medication:

_____

_____

Changes in Behaviour:

_____

_____

Notes:

_____

_____

### Vet Check Up Appointments:

_____          _____

_____          _____

_____          _____

_____          _____

# My Chicken's
# HEALTH

## Health Record

Date:

Condition/Illness/Symptoms:

_____

_____

Treatment/Medication:

_____

_____

Changes in Behaviour:

_____

_____

Notes:

_____

_____

## Vet Check Up Appointments:

_____          _____

_____          _____

_____          _____

_____          _____

# My Chicken's
# HEALTH

Health Record

Date:

Condition/Illness/Symptoms:

_____

_____

Treatment/Medication:

_____

_____

Changes in Behaviour:

_____

_____

Notes:

_____

_____

Vet Check Up Appointments:

_____        _____

_____        _____

_____        _____

_____        _____

# My Chicken's
# HEALTH

Health Record

Date:

Condition/Illness/Symptoms:

_____

_____

Treatment/Medication:

_____

_____

Changes in Behaviour:

_____

_____

Notes:

_____

_____

Vet Check Up Appointments:

_____          _____

_____          _____

_____          _____

_____          _____

# My Chicken's
# HEALTH

## Health Record

Date:

Condition/Illness/Symptoms:

_____

_____

Treatment/Medication:

_____

_____

Changes in Behaviour:

_____

_____

Notes:

_____

_____

## Vet Check Up Appointments:

_____          _____

_____          _____

_____          _____

_____          _____

# My Chicken's
# HEALTH

## Health Record

Date:

Condition/Illness/Symptoms:

_____

_____

Treatment/Medication:

_____

_____

Changes in Behaviour:

_____

_____

Notes:

_____

_____

## Vet Check Up Appointments:

_____          _____

_____          _____

_____          _____

_____          _____

# Notes &
# OBSERVATIONS

_____

_____

_____

_____

_____

_____

_____

_____

_____

_____

_____

_____

_____

 # My CHICKEN

*Place a Picture of Your Chicken Here*

# My
# CHICKEN

Name:

_____

_____

Breed/Type of Chicken:

_____

Date/Place of Purchase:

_____

Hen ☐                    Rooster ☐

Purpose:  ☐Egg Layer  ☐Meat  ☐Pet  ☐Other

Description/Colors/Identifying Marks:

_____

_____

Known Age/Hatch Date:

_____

Diet/Feed Type:

_____

_____

Notes

_____

_____

_____

# My Chicken's
# HEALTH

Health Record

Date:

Condition/Illness/Symptoms:

_____

_____

Treatment/Medication:

_____

_____

Changes in Behaviour:

_____

_____

Notes:

_____

_____

Vet Check Up Appointments:

_____          _____

_____          _____

_____          _____

_____          _____

# My Chicken's
# HEALTH

## Health Record

Date:

Condition/Illness/Symptoms:

_____

_____

Treatment/Medication:

_____

_____

Changes in Behaviour:

_____

_____

Notes:

_____

_____

## Vet Check Up Appointments:

_____          _____

_____          _____

_____          _____

_____          _____

# My Chicken's
# HEALTH

## Health Record

Date:

Condition/Illness/Symptoms:

_____

_____

Treatment/Medication:

_____

_____

Changes in Behaviour:

_____

_____

Notes:

_____

_____

### Vet Check Up Appointments:

_____          _____

_____          _____

_____          _____

_____          _____

 My Chicken's
# HEALTH

Health Record

Date:

Condition/Illness/Symptoms:

_____

_____

Treatment/Medication:

_____

_____

Changes in Behaviour:

_____

_____

Notes:

_____

_____

Vet Check Up Appointments:

_____          _____

_____          _____

_____          _____

_____          _____

# My Chicken's
# HEALTH

Health Record

Date:

Condition/Illness/Symptoms:

_____

_____

Treatment/Medication:

_____

_____

Changes in Behaviour:

_____

_____

Notes:

_____

_____

Vet Check Up Appointments:

_____          _____

_____          _____

_____          _____

_____          _____

# My Chicken's
# HEALTH

Health Record

Date:

Condition/Illness/Symptoms:

_____

_____

Treatment/Medication:

_____

_____

Changes in Behaviour:

_____

_____

Notes:

_____

_____

Vet Check Up Appointments:

_____        _____

_____        _____

_____        _____

_____        _____

# My Chicken's
# HEALTH

## Health Record

Date:

Condition/Illness/Symptoms:

_____

_____

Treatment/Medication:

_____

_____

Changes in Behaviour:

_____

_____

Notes:

_____

_____

## Vet Check Up Appointments:

_____          _____

_____          _____

_____          _____

_____          _____

# My Chicken's
# HEALTH

## Health Record

Date:

Condition/Illness/Symptoms:

_____

_____

Treatment/Medication:

_____

_____

Changes in Behaviour:

_____

_____

Notes:

_____

_____

## Vet Check Up Appointments:

_____          _____

_____          _____

_____          _____

_____          _____

# My Chicken's
# HEALTH

Health Record

Date:

Condition/Illness/Symptoms:

_____

_____

Treatment/Medication:

_____

_____

Changes in Behaviour:

_____

_____

Notes:

_____

_____

Vet Check Up Appointments:

_____          _____

_____          _____

_____          _____

_____          _____

# My Chicken's
# HEALTH

## Health Record

Date:

Condition/Illness/Symptoms:

_____

_____

Treatment/Medication:

_____

_____

Changes in Behaviour:

_____

_____

Notes:

_____

_____

## Vet Check Up Appointments:

_____          _____

_____          _____

_____          _____

_____          _____

# Notes &
# OBSERVATIONS

# My
# CHICKEN

*Place a Picture of Your Chicken Here*

# My
# CHICKEN

Name:

_____

_____

Breed/Type of Chicken:

_____

Date/Place of Purchase:

_____

Hen ☐                    Rooster ☐

Purpose: ☐Egg Layer  ☐Meat  ☐Pet  ☐Other

Description/Colors/Identifying Marks:

_____

_____

Known Age/Hatch Date:

_____

Diet/Feed Type:

_____

_____

Notes

_____

_____

_____

# My Chicken's
# HEALTH

### Health Record

Date:

Condition/Illness/Symptoms:

_____

_____

Treatment/Medication:

_____

_____

Changes in Behaviour:

_____

_____

Notes:

_____

_____

### Vet Check Up Appointments:

_____     _____

_____     _____

_____     _____

_____     _____

# My Chicken's
# HEALTH

Health Record

Date:

Condition/Illness/Symptoms:

_____

_____

Treatment/Medication:

_____

_____

Changes in Behaviour:

_____

_____

Notes:

_____

_____

Vet Check Up Appointments:

_____          _____

_____          _____

_____          _____

_____          _____

# My Chicken's
# HEALTH

## Health Record

Date:

Condition/Illness/Symptoms:

_____

_____

Treatment/Medication:

_____

_____

Changes in Behaviour:

_____

_____

Notes:

_____

_____

## Vet Check Up Appointments:

_____        _____

_____        _____

_____        _____

_____        _____

# My Chicken's
# HEALTH

Health Record

Date:

Condition/Illness/Symptoms:

_____

_____

Treatment/Medication:

_____

_____

Changes in Behaviour:

_____

_____

Notes:

_____

_____

Vet Check Up Appointments:

_____          _____

_____          _____

_____          _____

_____          _____

# My Chicken's
# HEALTH

## Health Record

Date:

Condition/Illness/Symptoms:

_____

_____

Treatment/Medication:

_____

_____

Changes in Behaviour:

_____

_____

Notes:

_____

_____

### Vet Check Up Appointments:

_____          _____

_____          _____

_____          _____

_____          _____

# My Chicken's
# HEALTH

*Health Record*

Date:

Condition/Illness/Symptoms:

_____

_____

Treatment/Medication:

_____

_____

Changes in Behaviour:

_____

_____

Notes:

_____

_____

Vet Check Up Appointments:

_____          _____

_____          _____

_____          _____

_____          _____

 My Chicken's
# HEALTH

## Health Record

Date:

Condition/Illness/Symptoms:

_____

_____

Treatment/Medication:

_____

_____

Changes in Behaviour:

_____

_____

Notes:

_____

_____

## Vet Check Up Appointments:

_____        _____

_____        _____

_____        _____

_____        _____

# My Chicken's
# HEALTH

### Health Record

Date:

Condition/Illness/Symptoms:

_____

_____

Treatment/Medication:

_____

_____

Changes in Behaviour:

_____

_____

Notes:

_____

_____

### Vet Check Up Appointments:

_____        _____

_____        _____

_____        _____

_____        _____

# My Chicken's
# HEALTH

Health Record

Date:

Condition/Illness/Symptoms:

_____

_____

Treatment/Medication:

_____

_____

Changes in Behaviour:

_____

_____

Notes:

_____

_____

Vet Check Up Appointments:

_____     _____

_____     _____

_____     _____

_____     _____

# My Chicken's
# HEALTH

### Health Record

Date:

Condition/Illness/Symptoms:

_____

_____

Treatment/Medication:

_____

_____

Changes in Behaviour:

_____

_____

Notes:

_____

_____

### Vet Check Up Appointments:

_____          _____

_____          _____

_____          _____

_____          _____

# Notes &
# OBSERVATIONS

# My
# CHICKEN

*Place a Picture of Your Chicken Here*

# My
# CHICKEN

Name:

_____

_____

Breed/Type of Chicken:

_____

Date/Place of Purchase:

_____

Hen ☐                                    Rooster ☐

Purpose: ☐Egg Layer  ☐Meat  ☐Pet  ☐Other

Description/Colors/Identifying Marks:

_____

_____

Known Age/Hatch Date:

_____

Diet/Feed Type:

_____

_____

Notes

_____

_____

_____

# My Chicken's
# HEALTH

## Health Record

Date:

Condition/Illness/Symptoms:

_____

_____

Treatment/Medication:

_____

_____

Changes in Behaviour:

_____

_____

Notes:

_____

_____

### Vet Check Up Appointments:

_____        _____

_____        _____

_____        _____

_____        _____

 My Chicken's **HEALTH**

## Health Record

Date:

Condition/Illness/Symptoms:

_____

_____

Treatment/Medication:

_____

_____

Changes in Behaviour:

_____

_____

Notes:

_____

_____

## Vet Check Up Appointments:

_____     _____

_____     _____

_____     _____

_____     _____

 # My Chicken's
# HEALTH

## Health Record

Date:

Condition/Illness/Symptoms:

_____

_____

Treatment/Medication:

_____

_____

Changes in Behaviour:

_____

_____

Notes:

_____

_____

## Vet Check Up Appointments:

_____        _____

_____        _____

_____        _____

_____        _____

 My Chicken's

# HEALTH

*Health Record*

Date:

Condition/Illness/Symptoms:

_____

_____

Treatment/Medication:

_____

_____

Changes in Behaviour:

_____

_____

Notes:

_____

_____

*Vet Check Up Appointments:*

_____        _____

_____        _____

_____        _____

_____        _____

# My Chicken's
# HEALTH

Health Record

Date:

Condition/Illness/Symptoms:

_____

_____

Treatment/Medication:

_____

_____

Changes in Behaviour:

_____

_____

Notes:

_____

_____

Vet Check Up Appointments:

_____          _____

_____          _____

_____          _____

_____          _____

 # My Chicken's
# HEALTH

## Health Record

Date:

Condition/Illness/Symptoms:

_____

_____

Treatment/Medication:

_____

_____

Changes in Behaviour:

_____

_____

Notes:

_____

_____

## Vet Check Up Appointments:

_____          _____

_____          _____

_____          _____

_____          _____

# My Chicken's
# HEALTH

Health Record

Date:

Condition/Illness/Symptoms:

_____

_____

Treatment/Medication:

_____

_____

Changes in Behaviour:

_____

_____

Notes:

_____

_____

Vet Check Up Appointments:

_____          _____

_____          _____

_____          _____

_____          _____

# My Chicken's
# HEALTH

### Health Record

Date:

Condition/Illness/Symptoms:

_____

_____

Treatment/Medication:

_____

_____

Changes in Behaviour:

_____

_____

Notes:

_____

_____

### Vet Check Up Appointments:

_____         _____

_____         _____

_____         _____

_____         _____

# My Chicken's
# HEALTH

Health Record

Date:

Condition/Illness/Symptoms:

_____

_____

Treatment/Medication:

_____

_____

Changes in Behaviour:

_____

_____

Notes:

_____

_____

Vet Check Up Appointments:

_____          _____

_____          _____

_____          _____

_____          _____

# My Chicken's
# HEALTH

## Health Record

Date:

Condition/Illness/Symptoms:

_____

_____

Treatment/Medication:

_____

_____

Changes in Behaviour:

_____

_____

Notes:

_____

_____

### Vet Check Up Appointments:

_____     _____

_____     _____

_____     _____

_____     _____

# Notes &
# OBSERVATIONS

 # My
# CHICKEN

*Place a Picture of Your Chicken Here*

 My
# CHICKEN

Name:
_____

_____

Breed/Type of Chicken:
_____

Date/Place of Purchase:
_____

Hen ☐                                    Rooster ☐

Purpose: ☐Egg Layer  ☐Meat  ☐Pet  ☐Other

Description/Colors/Identifying Marks:
_____

_____

Known Age/Hatch Date:
_____

Diet/Feed Type:

_____

_____

Notes

_____

_____

_____

# My Chicken's
# HEALTH

## Health Record

Date:

Condition/Illness/Symptoms:

_____

_____

Treatment/Medication:

_____

_____

Changes in Behaviour:

_____

_____

Notes:

_____

_____

### Vet Check Up Appointments:

_____          _____

_____          _____

_____          _____

_____          _____

# My Chicken's
# HEALTH

Health Record

Date:

Condition/Illness/Symptoms:

_____
_____

Treatment/Medication:

_____
_____

Changes in Behaviour:

_____
_____

Notes:

_____
_____

Vet Check Up Appointments:

_____        _____

_____        _____

_____        _____

_____        _____

# My Chicken's
# HEALTH

### Health Record

Date:

Condition/Illness/Symptoms:

_____

_____

Treatment/Medication:

_____

_____

Changes in Behaviour:

_____

_____

Notes:

_____

_____

### Vet Check Up Appointments:

_____          _____

_____          _____

_____          _____

_____          _____

 # My Chicken's
# HEALTH

### Health Record

Date:

Condition/Illness/Symptoms:

_____

_____

Treatment/Medication:

_____

_____

Changes in Behaviour:

_____

_____

Notes:

_____

_____

### Vet Check Up Appointments:

_____         _____

_____         _____

_____         _____

_____         _____

# My Chicken's
# HEALTH

### Health Record

Date:

Condition/Illness/Symptoms:

_____

_____

Treatment/Medication:

_____

_____

Changes in Behaviour:

_____

_____

Notes:

_____

_____

### Vet Check Up Appointments:

_____         _____

_____         _____

_____         _____

_____         _____

# My Chicken's
# HEALTH

Health Record

Date:

Condition/Illness/Symptoms:
_____
_____

Treatment/Medication:
_____
_____

Changes in Behaviour:
_____
_____

Notes:
_____
_____

Vet Check Up Appointments:

_____          _____

_____          _____

_____          _____

_____          _____

# My Chicken's
# HEALTH

### Health Record

Date:

Condition/Illness/Symptoms:

_____

_____

Treatment/Medication:

_____

_____

Changes in Behaviour:

_____

_____

Notes:

_____

_____

### Vet Check Up Appointments:

_____     _____

_____     _____

_____     _____

_____     _____

 # My Chicken's
# HEALTH

## Health Record

Date:

Condition/Illness/Symptoms:

_____

_____

Treatment/Medication:

_____

_____

Changes in Behaviour:

_____

_____

Notes:

_____

_____

## Vet Check Up Appointments:

_____        _____

_____        _____

_____        _____

_____        _____

 # My Chicken's
# HEALTH

## Health Record

Date:

Condition/Illness/Symptoms:

_____

_____

Treatment/Medication:

_____

_____

Changes in Behaviour:

_____

_____

Notes:

_____

_____

## Vet Check Up Appointments:

_____        _____

_____        _____

_____        _____

_____        _____

# My Chicken's
# HEALTH

Health Record

Date:

Condition/Illness/Symptoms:

_____

_____

Treatment/Medication:

_____

_____

Changes in Behaviour:

_____

_____

Notes:

_____

_____

Vet Check Up Appointments:

_____         _____

_____         _____

_____         _____

_____         _____

# Notes &
# OBSERVATIONS

_____

_____

_____

_____

_____

_____

_____

_____

_____

_____

_____

_____

_____

_____

# My
# CHICKEN

*Place a Picture of Your Chicken Here*

 # My
# CHICKEN

Name:
_____

_____

Breed/Type of Chicken:
_____

Date/Place of Purchase:
_____

Hen ☐                    Rooster ☐

Purpose: ☐Egg Layer  ☐Meat  ☐Pet  ☐Other

Description/Colors/Identifying Marks:
_____

_____

Known Age/Hatch Date:
_____

Diet/Feed Type:
_____

_____

Notes
_____

_____

_____

# My Chicken's
# HEALTH

Health Record

Date:

Condition/Illness/Symptoms:

_____

_____

Treatment/Medication:

_____

_____

Changes in Behaviour:

_____

_____

Notes:

_____

_____

Vet Check Up Appointments:

_____     _____

_____     _____

_____     _____

_____     _____

# My Chicken's
# HEALTH

### Health Record

Date:

Condition/Illness/Symptoms:

_____

_____

Treatment/Medication:

_____

_____

Changes in Behaviour:

_____

_____

Notes:

_____

_____

### Vet Check Up Appointments:

_____     _____

_____     _____

_____     _____

_____     _____

# My Chicken's
# HEALTH

Health Record

Date:

Condition/Illness/Symptoms:

_____

_____

Treatment/Medication:

_____

_____

Changes in Behaviour:

_____

_____

Notes:

_____

_____

Vet Check Up Appointments:

_____        _____

_____        _____

_____        _____

_____        _____

# My Chicken's
# HEALTH

## Health Record

Date:

Condition/Illness/Symptoms:

_____

_____

Treatment/Medication:

_____

_____

Changes in Behaviour:

_____

_____

Notes:

_____

_____

## Vet Check Up Appointments:

_____     _____

_____     _____

_____     _____

_____     _____

# My Chicken's
# HEALTH

Health Record

Date:

Condition/Illness/Symptoms:

_____

_____

Treatment/Medication:

_____

_____

Changes in Behaviour:

_____

_____

Notes:

_____

_____

Vet Check Up Appointments:

_____          _____

_____          _____

_____          _____

_____          _____

# My Chicken's
# HEALTH

Health Record

Date:

Condition/Illness/Symptoms:

_____

_____

Treatment/Medication:

_____

_____

Changes in Behaviour:

_____

_____

Notes:

_____

_____

Vet Check Up Appointments:

_____          _____

_____          _____

_____          _____

_____          _____

# My Chicken's
# HEALTH

## Health Record

Date:

Condition/Illness/Symptoms:

_____

_____

Treatment/Medication:

_____

_____

Changes in Behaviour:

_____

_____

Notes:

_____

_____

### Vet Check Up Appointments:

_____          _____

_____          _____

_____          _____

_____          _____

# My Chicken's
# HEALTH

## Health Record

Date:

Condition/Illness/Symptoms:

_____

_____

Treatment/Medication:

_____

_____

Changes in Behaviour:

_____

_____

Notes:

_____

_____

### Vet Check Up Appointments:

_____        _____

_____        _____

_____        _____

_____        _____

# My Chicken's
# HEALTH

## Health Record

Date:

Condition/Illness/Symptoms:

_____

_____

Treatment/Medication:

_____

_____

Changes in Behaviour:

_____

_____

Notes:

_____

_____

## Vet Check Up Appointments:

_____        _____

_____        _____

_____        _____

_____        _____

# My Chicken's
# HEALTH

### Health Record

Date:

Condition/Illness/Symptoms:

_____

_____

Treatment/Medication:

_____

_____

Changes in Behaviour:

_____

_____

Notes:

_____

_____

### Vet Check Up Appointments:

_____        _____

_____        _____

_____        _____

_____        _____

# Notes &
# OBSERVATIONS

 # My
# CHICKEN

Place a Picture of Your Chicken Here

# My
# CHICKEN

Name:

_____

_____

Breed/Type of Chicken:

_____

Date/Place of Purchase:

_____

Hen ☐          Rooster ☐

Purpose: ☐Egg Layer   ☐Meat   ☐Pet   ☐Other

Description/Colors/Identifying Marks:

_____

_____

Known Age/Hatch Date:

_____

Diet/Feed Type:

_____

_____

Notes

_____

_____

_____

# My Chicken's
# HEALTH

## Health Record

Date:

Condition/Illness/Symptoms:

_____

_____

Treatment/Medication:

_____

_____

Changes in Behaviour:

_____

_____

Notes:

_____

_____

### Vet Check Up Appointments:

_____          _____

_____          _____

_____          _____

_____          _____

# My Chicken's
# HEALTH

Health Record

Date:

Condition/Illness/Symptoms:

_____

_____

Treatment/Medication:

_____

_____

Changes in Behaviour:

_____

_____

Notes:

_____

_____

Vet Check Up Appointments:

_____          _____

_____          _____

_____          _____

_____          _____

# My Chicken's
# HEALTH

## Health Record

Date:

Condition/Illness/Symptoms:

_____

_____

Treatment/Medication:

_____

_____

Changes in Behaviour:

_____

_____

Notes:

_____

_____

## Vet Check Up Appointments:

_____        _____

_____        _____

_____        _____

_____        _____

# My Chicken's
# HEALTH

### Health Record

Date:

Condition/Illness/Symptoms:

_____

_____

Treatment/Medication:

_____

_____

Changes in Behaviour:

_____

_____

Notes:

_____

_____

### Vet Check Up Appointments:

_____     _____

_____     _____

_____     _____

_____     _____

# My Chicken's
# HEALTH

## Health Record

Date:

Condition/Illness/Symptoms:

_____

_____

Treatment/Medication:

_____

_____

Changes in Behaviour:

_____

_____

Notes:

_____

_____

## Vet Check Up Appointments:

_____        _____

_____        _____

_____        _____

_____        _____

 # My Chicken's
# HEALTH

## Health Record

Date:

Condition/Illness/Symptoms:

_____

_____

Treatment/Medication:

_____

_____

Changes in Behaviour:

_____

_____

Notes:

_____

_____

## Vet Check Up Appointments:

_____          _____

_____          _____

_____          _____

_____          _____

# My Chicken's
# HEALTH

## Health Record

Date:

Condition/Illness/Symptoms:

_____

_____

Treatment/Medication:

_____

_____

Changes in Behaviour:

_____

_____

Notes:

_____

_____

## Vet Check Up Appointments:

_____        _____

_____        _____

_____        _____

_____        _____

# My Chicken's
# HEALTH

Health Record

Date:

Condition/Illness/Symptoms:

_____

_____

Treatment/Medication:

_____

_____

Changes in Behaviour:

_____

_____

Notes:

_____

_____

Vet Check Up Appointments:

_____          _____

_____          _____

_____          _____

_____          _____

# My Chicken's
# HEALTH

### Health Record

Date:

Condition/Illness/Symptoms:

_____

_____

Treatment/Medication:

_____

_____

Changes in Behaviour:

_____

_____

Notes:

_____

_____

### Vet Check Up Appointments:

_____        _____

_____        _____

_____        _____

_____        _____

# My Chicken's
# HEALTH

Health Record

Date:

Condition/Illness/Symptoms:

_____

_____

Treatment/Medication:

_____

_____

Changes in Behaviour:

_____

_____

Notes:

_____

_____

Vet Check Up Appointments:

_____        _____

_____        _____

_____        _____

_____        _____

# Notes &
# OBSERVATIONS

_____

_____

_____

_____

_____

_____

_____

_____

_____

_____

_____

_____

_____

_____

www.ingramcontent.com/pod-product-compliance
Lightning Source LLC
Chambersburg PA
CBHW081400280526
45788CB00009B/2941